797,885 Books
are available to read at

Forgotten Books

www.ForgottenBooks.com

Forgotten Books' App
Available for mobile, tablet & eReader

ISBN 978-1-333-31888-8
PIBN 10489304

This book is a reproduction of an important historical work. Forgotten Books uses
state-of-the-art technology to digitally reconstruct the work, preserving the original format
whilst repairing imperfections present in the aged copy. In rare cases, an imperfection in
the original, such as a blemish or missing page, may be replicated in our edition. We do,
however, repair the vast majority of imperfections successfully; any imperfections that
remain are intentionally left to preserve the state of such historical works.

Forgotten Books is a registered trademark of FB &c Ltd.
Copyright © 2017 FB &c Ltd.
FB &c Ltd, Dalton House, 60 Windsor Avenue, London, SW19 2RR.
Company number 08720141. Registered in England and Wales.

For support please visit www.forgottenbooks.com

1 MONTH OF FREE READING

at
www.ForgottenBooks.com

By purchasing this book you are eligible for one month membership to ForgottenBooks.com, giving you unlimited access to our entire collection of over 700,000 titles via our web site and mobile apps.

To claim your free month visit:
www.forgottenbooks.com/free489304

* Offer is valid for 45 days from date of purchase. Terms and conditions apply.

English
Français
Deutsche
Italiano
Español
Português

www.forgottenbooks.com

Mythology Photography **Fiction** Fishing Christianity **Art** Cooking Essays Buddhism Freemasonry Medicine **Biology** Music **Ancient Egypt** Evolution Carpentry Physics Dance Geology **Mathematics** Fitness Shakespeare **Folklore** Yoga Marketing **Confidence** Immortality Biographies Poetry **Psychology** Witchcraft Electronics Chemistry History **Law** Accounting **Philosophy** Anthropology Alchemy Drama Quantum Mechanics Atheism Sexual Health **Ancient History Entrepreneurship** Languages Sport Paleontology Needlework Islam **Metaphysics** Investment Archaeology Parenting Statistics Criminology **Motivational**

PREFACE.

In compliance with the wishes of his relatives and friends, the author of the following lines has consented to the collection and publication of such of his productions in verse as are deemed worthy of preservation. They are not many nor of a sufficiently high order to be designated as poems, yet may not be altogether without some value as keepsakes. Should their perusal afford the reader a tithe of the pleasure that their composition gave the writer, then will have been accomplished all that may reasonably be expected by   THE AUTHOR,

William Hazeltine.

CONTENTS.

	Page.
A Dream of Youth.	1.
On the Death of a Friend.	3.
The Web of Life.	4.
At the River.	5.
Life.	6.
The New Year.	7.
"Follow Thou Me."	7.
The Torn Leaf.	9.
Groping in the Dark.	9.
Rescued.	10.
A Simile.	10.
At Pacific Grove.	11.
The Secret.	12.
The Voice of the Morning.	13.
Grandmother.	13.
Lege Spiritus.	14.
This Old Back Yard of Ours.	15.
The Nativity.	17.
A Plea for Children.	18.
The Parson's Text.	19.
Barred.	19.
Something Wrong.	20.
To One Absent.	21.
The Latest Song.	21.
The Dawn of Peace.	23.
Raindrops.	23.
In Dream-land.	24.
Immortality.	25.
The Butternut Tree by the Brook.	26.
That "Dumb Terror."	27

RANDOM RHYMES.

A DREAM OF YOUTH.

I slept. I dreamed. Methought, a boy again,
I roamed o'er hill and field and flowery plain;
'Mong sunny bowers; beside the rippling rill
That danced in glee adown the mossy hill;
Along old paths, beside familiar rocks
Where oft, in youth, I watched my father's flocks.
   Methought I saw the same old cot that stood.
Close by the merry, music-haunted wood;
And wandered through its halls, a child again,
And listened to the old familiar strain
My mother sang while swinging swift the reel
That gathered from the spindle of the wheel
Threads blue and white. And then I stood beside
My father pleading for a "pig-back" ride
Just round the corner by the towering stack,
When, with a laugh, he placed me on his back
And cantered off with all his manly mien,
While mother, from the window, watched the scene.
   Again methought along the grassy shore
Of babbling brook I wandered, as of yore,
While ever and anon the timid trout,
Alarmed at my advances, darted out
To seek some other quiet, lone retreat,

Beyond the jarring of intruding feet.
  The same old mound, within the meadow, where
A century past, have been preserved with care
The rough-hewn stones that mark the lonely bed
Of maid and sire met my advancing tread.
  I saw the elm that stood above the spring,
And in its branches hung the same old swing
I prized so much in youth—in days gone by—
And with a happy, wild, exultant cry,
I leaped upon the board to ride again
Like bird upon the air. My giddy brain
Lost all its nerve; 1 fell; and, with a scream,
Awoke to find 'twas but an idle dream.
  1859.

ON THE DEATH OF A FRIEND.

Ah, Death! why stretch thy ruthless hand
And pluck from out our social band
So bright a bud, just set to bloom,
And lay within the silent tomb?
Oh, is it true! and can it be
That one so full of life, that she,
The fondest of our little band,
Has gone—gone to the spirit land?
   That voice we loved so oft to hear
Ring forth in accents sweet and clear,
No more will lend its charms to ease
A suffering world, nor yet to please
The willing ear of such as throng
To hear the sweeter chords of song.
   Farewell, loved one! from us departed;
So loving, generous and true-hearted;
Yet memory lives to shed a tear
For thee we loved and prized so dear.
Farewell! On earth we meet no more;
Yet we may hope, 'yond Jordan's shore,
To meet thee there and hear again
Thy voice in never-ending strain,
Made perfect now, in Christ above,
To sing His everlasting love.

THE WEB OF LIFE.

A weaver sat weaving a web of life.
   As he labored, with patient care,
I minded his scanty locks were rife
   With many a silvery hair.

"What do you here, good toiler," I said,
   "You seem to be sorely tried ;
What signifies all this confusion of thread ?"
   To which the weaver replied :

"This web is composed of a warp and woof,
   And I weave them together, so;"
And with skillful hand the weaver, for proof,
   Threw his shuttle-stick to and fro.

"These threads," he resumed, "are what we term
   The warp, or, in other phrase,
"The 'Natural Man,' and we trace their germ
   Far back to primeval days.

"The woof is a texture of intricate hue,
   And threads from necessity spun ;
Art, Science, Religion, these serve to endue
   It with strength, and combine it in one."

And the weaver wove his Web of Life,
   And his face was furrowed with care ;
While his locks, as he bent in the toilsome strife,
   Showed many a silvery hair.

AT THE RIVER.

Cold hang the mists over Jordan's dark billow,
   Weeping I stand on the shadowy shore,
Wet with the dew-drops that fall from the willow,
   Listening the dip of the mystical oar.

Words are but idle, arranged though in numbers;
   Earth has no language befitting, at best,
The expressions of peace I could wish to the slumbers
   Of one who in Jesus is taking her rest.

Few are the years since, rejoicing, we started
   On life's hopeful journey together below ;
And now she is gone while I live, broken-hearted,
   To wander alone through this valley of woe.

Like tendrils of comfort around me are twining
   The arms of our darling and motherless one ;
A solace in sorrow too deep for repining ;
   A star that shines brighter when clouded the sun.

A little more sorrow, a little more sighing,
   A little more labor, a little more life,
And I too must know what it is to be dying,
   And sadly or joyfully give up the strife.

Though cold are the mists that encompass the billow,
   And dark be the shadows that rest on the shore ;
Waiting I stand 'neath the dew-dropping willow,
   And list the return of the mystical oar.

September 14, 1869.

LIFE.

Life is like a widening river,
   Flowing onward to the sea,
There its waters to deliver
To the great and all-wise giver—
                Deity.

We commence its varied journey
   Through the little laughing rill,
Growing on whose banks are flowers,
Bidding us these hands of ours
                well to fill.

Grasp we at them as, in passing,
   We behold them very near,
Opening to the sunbeams early,
Sparkling now with dewdrops pearly,
                bright and clear.

Happy we if, when the river
   Wider, deeper, darker grows;
And the distant shores no longer
Seem to check it as it stronger,
                sterner flows;

And the trees upon its margin
   Bloom no more for you and me,
We shall find these hands of ours
Laden with its choicest flowers,
                happy we.

THE NEW YEAR.

Since yestereve Time's hour-glass has made
Another turn—its sands again obeyed
The sure decree of Him whose fiat just
Went forth with man's creation from the dust.

Upon the threshold of a new-born year
Again we stand, and list, with fancy's ear,
The old year's requiem, rehearsed once more
By moaning night-winds through the forest hoar.

Another leaf in life's eventful book
Is turned. How solemn! Yet with those who look
Beyond this mortal, as by Jesus taught,
Is joy well mingled with the solemn thought.

The virgin page, unspotted yet and bright,
Is now before us. On it let us write
In letters golden that may brighter grow
With each succeeding year we trace below.

1870.

"FOLLOW THOU ME."

When, how or where a sinful race
   Shall find their just reward,
Has naught to do with his free grace,
   Why trouble ye my Lord
With speculative thoughts that serve
   No useful purpose here

8.

To bind our hearts in closer love,
   Or banish e'en a fear.

It is enough for me to know
   If I the prize receive
Which Jesus purchased to bestow
   On such as should believe,
I must not lag at every hill
   With idle men to talk,
But seek to learn my Master's will,
   And in his footsteps walk.

THE TORN LEAF.

She tore it—Alice tore it,
  And now, with childish grief,
To me she quickly bore it—
  The sad, disfigured leaf.

She did not mean to bend it
  So hard, and that was why
She asked if I could mend it:
  "Yes, darling, I will try."

The tattered leaf I could not
  So easily restore;
And now, though torn, I would not
  Have it as 'twas before.

Have you no darling Alice
  Whose absence here you mourn;
No keepsakes in your palace;
  No leaves that have been torn?

GROPING IN THE DARK.

Kind reader, did you ever have
  Occasion in the night
To feel your way through door ajar,
  Unaided by the light;
And when you thought the coast was clear,
  Still feeling out before,
You ran your face square on the edge
  Of some half-open door?

Well, such is life. How much we grope
  In moral darkness here,
Unaided by the Gospel light
  To make our pathway clear
And save us many bruises that
  Are sure to leave a scar,
From running blindly 'gainst the doors
  That sin has left ajar.

RESCUED.

A sun-beam met a breeze one summer day,
  And poised a shaft to strike the zephyr's heart,
When quickly sprang a shadow in the way,
  And caught upon its shield the hurtling dart.

A SIMILE.

Fragments of good that strew life's stormy sea
  Are like the twigs that drift on ocean's crest;—
  Glad messages from God of home and rest,
Where faith is swallowed up in victory.

AT PACIFIC GROVE.

A broad deep bay before my vision lies,
O'er which the tilting, white-winged shallop flies;
Its waves are with the leaning sunbeams lit,
And wild birds o'er its dimpled bosom flit.

E'er empire's star here shed her golden light
The red man roamed in undisputed right,
And blindly offered, when the day was done,
His adorations to the setting sun.

A restful cadence fills the brooding air
To woo the weary from a life of care;
While time lies slumbering in an evermore
Of drowsy ripples lapsing on the shore.

With aimless tread we wander here and there
'Mong jagged and unshapely ledges, where
Strange beings of the sea insensate dwell,
Repletely nourished by the reaching swell.

From lodgments, fashioned by the hand of time—
Pausing to ponder on the scene sublime,
And count our blessings by the grains of sand
That lie, wave-washed, upon the ocean strand—

We hear the Angelus, with tender care,
Ring forth a summons to the house of prayer,
Where waiting father, faithful to his call,
Invokes a benediction over all.

THE SECRET.

I asked a man of wealth to tell me whence
   And what the secret of his worldly gain;
His answer was—"I simply save the pence
   And leave the pounds to rack another's brain."

I made inquiry of a man of lore
   To know the wherefore of his richer mind;
"In youth." he said "I gathered such a store
   Of choicer things as age might fail to find."

I importuned the Christian teacher how
   I best might gain that bliss beyond the grave;
He, smiling, said: "Twere well if I and thou
   Were mindful of the blessings that we have."

And thus I learned that he who would be rich
   Must not despise an honest penny earned;
That wisdom's garb is wrought with many a stitch,
   And joys immortal here on earth are learned.

THE VOICE OF THE MORNING.

Glad voice of the morning, how sweet are thy numbers,
　Dispelling the dew-mingled shadows away ;
As nature, refreshed, rises up from her slumbers,
　To welcome, with gladness, the dawning of day.

Oh voice of the morning, triumphantly breaking
　The stillness that hangs o'er the garden of gloom,
Rolls back the sealed stone while the Savior, awaking,
　Victorious walks through the door of the tomb.

Clear voice of that morning, how joyous thy numbers
　Will fall to the ears of the gathered above,
The plaudits who hear, risen up from their slumbers,
　" Well done, enter into the joy of thy love."

GRANDMOTHER.

How queer it seems to think that she
Was once a little Miss like me ;
And went to scool in crispy curls,
And laughed and played with other girls.

How odd to know that she could run
As we girls can, and have such fun
Repeating oft, in this our day,
The same old games she used to play.

So strange it sounds to hear her tell
When she was but a " gal," and dwell,
With kindling eye, on youthful themes,
When life was full of sunny dreams.

The dear old face is wrinkled now,
The dews of eve are on her brow;
She cannot do as once she could,
But we can love her just as good.

And if, when I am old and gray,
And gathering shadows dim the way,
A helping hand I then would find,
To her I must be ever kind.

LEGE SPIRITUS.

He who would lend a helping hand,
    But lacks wherewith to meet the need,
Has fully answered the demand
    By will, if not by deed.

Whoever would his fellow harm,
    Except the angry hand is stayed,
Though powerless be the pinioned arm,
    Still grasps the hilted blade.

To know the heart's inmost desire,
    Whatever be the purpose willed,
Is all that justice will require
    To prove the wish fulfilled.

THIS OLD BACK YARD OF OURS.

Let cultured bards, for golden gain,
    Employ their higher powers,
The while I sing, in silver strain,
    This old back yard of ours.

It is not large, nor yet so small
    But one finds plenteous way
To join, within its trellised wall,
    The children at their play.

For pastime purposes, a pile
    Of clean, gray ocean sand
Serves well in which to mold awhile
    Old castles, tall and grand.

A hammock, with well-anchored stays,
    Swings free beneath the trees---
A shady rest for those whose days
    Crave more of nature's ease.

A summer-house stands at one end,
    In which we often stay
To watch the boys make up and send
    Their mimic trains away.

Ruth skips the rope, and Ira wheels
    His baggage-wagon round,
While baby jerks her fists and heels
    To see the football bound.

A seesaw plank tilts up and down---
    A ship upon the sea,
Riding the waves to Ceylon's town
    To buy a load of tea.

And now a soldier prances nigh
   At a cavorting speed,
Touching his cap as he rides by
   Upon his broomstick steed.

Around the yard tall callas blow
   On tapering stems of green,
While near the gate low daisies grow,
   With chick-weed in between.

And when the shades of evening fall
   And darkness veils the day,
And 'round the hearth the children all
   Have gathered from their play,

Let others boast their broad parterres—
   Their choicer, rarer flowers,
I'll sing, 'mid duties evening cares,
   This old back yard of ours.

THE NATIVITY.

The sun had passed behind the Western Sea,
    The twilight stars shone dimly on the sight;
The ring-dove nestled in her favorite tree,
    And nature slumbered on the breast of night.

Now sought the flocks a kindly shelter where
    The rugged oak his leafy branches spread,
While shepherds watched their folds with tender care
    And listened for the wolf's disturbing tread.

From o'er the dim horizon of the east,
    Where earth and sky in dreamy distance lay,
The rising moon beamed softly through the mist
    To light the tardy herdsman on his way.

'Twas midnight in Judea, and lo! appeared,
    In shining robes, an angel from on high;
His face was radiant, and the shepherds feared
    And trembled lest some evil hovered nigh.

"Fear not," the angel said, "to you this morn—
    According to the ancient prophets's word—
In Bethlehem of Judea a child is born
    Of David's lineage, which is Christ the Lord.

"And this shall be to you a faithful sign:
    When, in a manger lying, ye shall see
A babe in swadling-bands among the kine,
    Know for a truth your promised Lord is He."

And suddenly through space was seen to fly
    A multitude of heavenly angels then,
Singing, "Glory, glory to our God most high,
    And peace upon the earth, good will toward men."

A PLEA FOR CHILDREN.

Speak to your child with cheerful voice,
   In accents sweet and calm;
'Twill make their little hearts rejoice,
   And act a soothing balm.

A balm for all their childish woes,
   A recompense for tears;
A shield from every blast that blows,
   A cordial for their fears.

'Twill be to them a solace sweet,
   As time, relentless, flies;
A rest to ease their weary feet;
   A pathway to the skies.

Utter no word of false alarm
   Their airy steps to stay;
Discourse no tale of future harm
   To spoil their happy play.

But rather fend them from the winds
   That chill their tender years;
And fill their young, receptive minds,
   With hopes instead of fears.

Kiss their soft cheeks of rosy hue,
   Smooth out their silken hair:
And with a mother's love bear you
   Their every trivial care.

THE PARSON'S TEXT.

Our little girl, of summers three,
   Had been instructed in the way
Of saying "thank you," if so be
   She might remember it to say.

One day the Parson, passing by,
   An orange gave the modest tot,
When shyly came the lisped reply:
   "Oh, hang you, thir; I moath fordot."

On next Lord's day the preacher read
   From 1st Corinthians, eleventh verse
And thirteenth chapter, which, he said,
   Would be the text for his discourse.

BARRED.

Seat me in no closed cathedral,
   Where true worshipers must wait for place;
Lay me rather at its portals
   With the weary, face to face.

Lay me where sweet carols mingle
   With the preacher's somnial prayer;
Lay me so fond echoes, endless,
   Lift me from a life of care.

Place me where some tear of gladness
   Glitters in God's diadem;
Where that tear at length may harden
   Into one eternal gem.

SOMETHING WRONG.

When we look out o'er this God-given world
    To see its inmates bound as with a thong ;
And hear loud words of mad invective hurled
    From man to man, we fear there's something wrong.

Considering all the haunts of sin and shame
    Which thrive unnoticed by the passing throng,
We sometimes wonder where to place the blame,
    Or who must answer for that something wrong.

When men stroll through our busy streets, in health,
    With downcast eyes and youthful sinews strong,
Knocking for favors at the doors of wealth,
    It almost seems that there is something wrong.

When we behold the gilded walls of sin
    That echo to some bacchanalian song,
And list the revelry by night within,
    We cannot else but think that something's wrong.

When greed and selfishness join hand in hand
    With wealth and power the conflict to prolong,
And men for gain will break the eighth command,
    I tell you what it is, there's something wrong.

TO ONE ABSENT.

In slumber oft I see thy smiling face
As one returned to her accustomed place;
And know not that in truth I do but dream,
So real doth thy fancied presence seem.

Yet though the vision may to me appear
So like to that sweet time when thou wert here,
I would not wish one moment to constrain
"Thy unbound spirit into bonds again."

Since last we parted, where the ebbing tide
Upon its bosom bore thee from my side,
Time has but illy served my grief to quell,
Although I know "He doeth all things well."

Though birds still carol, flitting to and fro,
Where lakelets lie and water-lilies blow,
"Somehow another world it seems to be"
Since last we parted by that mystic sea.

1890.

THE LATEST SONG.

Have you heard the latest song,
                    Uncle Sam,
Through dispatches from Hongkong,
                    by telegram ;
How our Dewey turned his tiller
For the harbor of Manila,
Sinking all of Spain's flotilla,
                    Uncle Sam ?

I tell you 'twas a daring
      thing at night,
Although the moon was staring
      down and bright,
 To steer his devious way
 Through a strange and foreign bay,
 To engage the Dons next day
      in a fight.

But Dewey's arm was steady,
      brave and true,
And he knew, when all was ready,
      what to do;
 So he sent his shells amain
 Through the battle-ships of Spain,
 Just in memory of the Maine
      and her crew.

" Yes, I've heard the latest song,"
      says Uncle Sam,
" Through dispatches from Hongkong,
      by cablegram,
 And I'll let my coat tails fly
 Till the last proud Don shall lie
 On fair Cuba's soil to die;
      am I a clam ?

THE DAWN OF PEACE.

Sweet smells the smoke of calumet to him
Who sees amid its circling waves some dim
Faint promise of a day when peace shall reign
Throughout the tropic isles of troubled Spain.

It is not ours the battle to prolong,
Beyond the righting of a flagrant wrong,
Nor yet to strike a super-added blow
In hatred of a fallen, bleeding foe.

Should Spain accept our generous terms of peace
To end the war and bid the conflict cease;
Then shall another picket-line be gained,
And nature's right to liberty sustained.

RAINDROPS.

They come; they come on wings of love,
    An angel host, in heaven's employ;
Swift heralds from the courts above,
    Bringing "good tidings of great joy."

They come; behold the countless throng
    As, earthward bound, they hover near
On mercy's errand, while their song
    Falls cheering on the shepherd's ear.

With thankful hearts we pause to hear
    The raindrops dripping from the eaves;
And see, or think we see, a year
    Before us rich in garnered sheaves.

IN DREAM-LAND.

Although 'twas but an idle dream I dreamed,
   A funnier one, may be, is seldom penned;
This way was something how the vision seemed,
   Especially when just about to end.

A funnier one, may be, is seldom penned,
   So full of inconsistences, and hence—
Especially when just about to end—
   So plainly destitute of common sense.

So full of inconsistences, and hence,
   To render safe some filthy lucre won,
So plainly destitute of common sense
   I started for a bank upon the run.

To render safe some filthy lucre won,
   Lest I might wake and fail to grasp the same,
I started for a bank upon the run
   To carry out my little greedy game.

Lest I might wake and fail to grasp the same,
   Although 'twas but an idle dream I dreamed,
To carry out my little greedy game,
   This way was something how the vision seemed.

25.

IMMORTALITY.

["It is," says Dr. Munger, "related of an Arab chief, whose laws forbade the rearing of his female offspring, that the only tears he ever shed were when his daughter brushed the dust from his beard as he buried her in a living grave."]

Well might the Arab, whose decree
   Refused protection to his child,
Bedew her grave with tears as she
   Looked up on him and smiled.

But where are shed the tears of God,
   As down to everlasting death
He backward thrusts the offered hands
   Outstretched to him in faith!

If death ends life, what is this world
   But one forever-yawning grave,
From which an ever-loving God
   His offspring cannot save.

THE BUTTERNUT TREE BY THE BROOK.

Does it stand there yet, that old home tree,
   Where rested the robin and rook,
As it stood in the days when it shaded me,
   By the banks of the rippling brook?

Does it stand there yet, that fruitful tree,
   Where the squirrel his forage took
From the boughs that stretched, in the sunlight free,
   Far out o'er the shadowy brook?

Does it stand there yet, as in autumn time,
   When the birds in their wisdom forsook
Its branches bare for a milder clime—
   That verdureless tree by the brook?

Long time has it braved the wintery storm,
   And oft in the cold blast shook;
Befriend it still, should its moldering form
   Lie prone by the muffled brook.

Ah! well hath my memory held the day
   When a last fond lingering look
I gave, as I turned from my home away,
   To that butternut tree by the brook.

THAT "DUMB TERROR."

[Suggested from reading Edwin Markham's "Man with the Hoe."]

With calloused hands, made strong by toil,
He grapples with the stubborn soil;
Nor looks to note each added name
Inscribed upon the scroll of fame.

Unmindful of the gulfs 'tween him
And the exalted seraphim,
A-field he goes for that he earns,
And at the "wheel of labor" turns.

With more to gain and less to lose,
No better calling may he choose
Than that where nature, his true friend,
A helping hand will surely lend.

Though scanty be his humble board,
He may, perhaps, have treasure stored
Where moth nor rust can leave their stains,
Nor thieves break through and steal his gains.

The wheel that turns within a wheel,
And has its given place to fill,
Was fashioned by the self-same mind
That in one whole all parts combined.

Not all on winged steeds may rise
To "peaks of song" amid the skies;
For some in dusty paths must find
The tasks for which they were designed.

And as for that "dumb terror," "stunned,"
That "soul-quenched" something to be shunned;
We know not if he has in art—
Much less in life—a counterpart.

Or great or small, or high or low,
From dust we came, to dust must go,
Where flowers of love alike will shed
Their fragrant petals o'er the dead.